A Crabtree Branches Book

eXtreme SPORTS
Kayaking

Bernard Conaghan

Crabtree Publishing
crabtreebooks.com

T0020256

School-to-Home Support for Caregivers and Teachers

This high-interest book is designed to motivate striving students with engaging topics while building fluency, vocabulary, and an interest in reading. Here are a few questions and activities to help the reader build upon his or her comprehension skills.

Before Reading:
- *What do I think this book is about?*
- *What do I know about this topic?*
- *What do I want to learn about this topic?*
- *Why am I reading this book?*

During Reading:
- *I wonder why...*
- *I'm curious to know...*
- *How is this like something I already know?*
- *What have I learned so far?*

After Reading:
- *What was the author trying to teach me?*
- *What are some details?*
- *How did the photographs and captions help me understand more?*
- *Read the book again and look for the vocabulary words.*
- *What questions do I still have?*

Extension Activities:
- *What was your favorite part of the book? Write a paragraph on it.*
- *Draw a picture of your favorite thing you learned from the book.*

Table of Contents

What Is Kayaking?

Kayaking is an **extreme** sport. A kayak is a small, narrow boat that is moved by using double-bladed paddles. Kayaking can be done on lakes, rivers, and other bodies of water. The kayak was invented more than 5,000 years ago by the **Indigenous** peoples of **arctic** North America.

Fun Fact

The word kayak means "hunter's boat."

Kayaking in Action

Kayaking is one of the most popular extreme sports in the world. There are many types of kayaking. Touring is a type of kayaking that is done on large bodies of water such as oceans or big lakes. These kayakers travel large distances over a long period of time.

Whitewater kayaking involves riding down rivers over fast-moving **rapids**. The power and speed of the rapids make this type of kayaking very exciting!

Fun Fact

Kayaking became an Olympic event in 1936.

Whitewater kayaking requires strength and balance. Some kayakers even go over waterfalls. In some whitewater competitions, kayakers paddle through gates.

Kayak surfing is a combination of whitewater kayaking and surfing. Instead of standing on a surfboard, kayakers are seated in their boats. They use rapids or waterfalls to do tricks. Some even use the ocean waves.

Fun Fact

The largest fish ever caught while kayak fishing was a 1,274-pound (578 kg) Greenland shark. It was caught by Joel Abrahamsson off the coast of Norway.

Some people enjoy using their kayaks to fish. Kayak fishing is often done in ponds, lakes, or streams. The kayak's size and shape allow it to reach places that a larger boat can't.

Where to Kayak

The most important part of kayaking is choosing where to kayak. For whitewater kayaking, it is important to find a fast-moving river with rapids. The Gauley River in West Virginia is one of the best in the world. For beginners, the San Juan River in Colorado is an excellent choice.

Gauley River, WV

San Juan River, CO

The Colorado River has areas for both calm paddling and fast whitewater kayaking. The steep **cliff** walls add to the beauty of the river.

Fun Fact

The Colorado River is one of the longest rivers in North America.

The Snake River is popular for kayak fishing. It also has exciting whitewater areas.

Parts of a Kayak

The top of the kayak is called the deck. The front is called the bow. The back of the boat is called the stern. The cockpit is the opening that has a seat where the rider sits. Thigh braces and foot braces help the kayaker control the boat.

Fun Fact

The fastest speed reached in a kayak is 19.2 miles per hour (30.9 km/h).

The bottom of the kayak is called the hull. It helps the boat stay **stable** in the water. A skeg or **rudder** is like a fin. It helps control the direction of the kayak.

Your Kayaking Career

The best way to become a kayaker is to go out on the water and start practicing. A coach can also be helpful. Once you've learned the basics of kayaking, a coach can also teach you important information about rivers, as well as safety tips such as how to do a kayak self-rescue.

If you become a good kayaker, you might be able to participate in the Extreme Kayak World Championship. This is a **tournament** that is held every summer. It includes many different kayaking events.

Kayaking Legends

Throughout the history of kayaking there have been many different **legends**. One of them is Jon Lugbill. He is a world champion, a one-time silver medal winner, and a seven-time member of a gold medal-winning team. He was born on May 27, 1961.

Fun Fact

Lugbill is the only athlete in history to have won 12 golds in the Whitewater World Championships.

Another kayaking legend is Nouria Newman. She won the Ottawa XL, a silver medal at the ICF Canoe Slalom World Championships, and the Extreme Kayaking World Championship. She also won team gold at the ICF Canoe Slalom World Championships and team bronze at the European Championships. She was born on September 9, 1991, in Chambéry, France.

Glossary

arctic (AARK-tik): The most northern region of Earth, including the North Pole and the area around it

cliff (KLIF): A high area of rock with a very steep side, often found near water

extreme (ek-STREEM): Something that is far beyond the normal

Indigenous (in-DIJ-ih-nuhs): The original inhabitants of a place

legend (LEH-jind): Someone who is famous and admired for doing something well

rapids (RA-pidz): A place in a river where the water flows very fast

rudder (RUH-der): A flat, movable piece, usually made of wood or metal, that is attached to a boat and is used for steering

stable (STEY-buhl): Not easily moved

tournament (TUR-nuh-ment): A competition with many participants

whitewater (WITE-waa-ter): Water in a river that moves very fast over rocks

Index

Websites to Visit

https://whitewater.org

https://olympics.com/en/sports/canoe-kayak-flatwater/

https://americancanoe.org

About the Author

Bernard Conaghan lives in South Carolina with his German shepherd named Duke. Every year he goes snowboarding in Switzerland. He is a coach on his son's football team. He always eats one scoop of peach ice cream after dinner.

Written by: Bernard Conaghan
Designed by: Jen Bowers
Series Development: James Earley
Proofreader: Melissa Boyce
Educational Consultant: Marie Lemke M.Ed.

Photographs: Cover image © 2010 VE.Studio/Shutterstock, background ©Matisson_ART/Shutterstock; p.3 & 17 ©2015 B Brown/Shutterstock; p.4 ©2010 VE.Studio/Shutterstock; p.6 ©2017 nadtochiy/Shutterstock; p.7 phone ©2017 Vasin Lee/Shutterstock, ©2018 Song_about_summer/Shutterstock; p.8 ©2014 Getmilitaryphotos/Shutterstock; p.9 ©2019 rightclickstudios/Shutterstock; p.11 ©2018 Artur Didyk/Shutterstock; p.12 ©2016 Kuznetcov_Konstantin/Shutterstock; p.14 ©2020 Arlene Waller/Shutterstock; p.15 ©2017 Andrej Safaric/Shutterstock; p.16 ©2012 Jim David/Shutterstock; p.18 ©2019 marekuliasz/Shutterstock; p.19 ©2018 Aleksandar Todorovic/Shutterstock; p.20 ©2011 Kris Schmidt/Shutterstock; p.22 ©2021 Nick Starichenko/Shutterstock; p.23 ©2019 Altrendo Images/Shutterstock; p.25 ©2019 Michele Morrone/Shutterstock; p.26 ©2020 Parilov/Shutterstock; p.27 medals © Net Vector/Shutterstock; p.29 © Ali Bharmal / Red Bull Content Pool

Crabtree Publishing

crabtreebooks.com   800-387-7650
Copyright © 2023 Crabtree Publishing

Printed in the U.S.A./012023/CG20220815

Published in Canada
Crabtree Publishing
616 Welland Avenue
St. Catharines, Ontario
L2M 5V6

Published in the United States
Crabtree Publishing
347 Fifth Avenue
Suite 1402-145
New York, New York 10016

Library and Archives Canada Cataloguing in Publication
Available at Library and Archives Canada

Library of Congress Cataloging-in-Publication Data
Available at the Library of Congress

Hardcover: 978-1-0396-9667-9
Paperback: 978-1-0396-9774-4
Ebook (pdf): 978-1-0396-9988-5
Epub: 978-1-0396-9881-9